To Pastor Rush

"Thank U Woman of God!"

AKS

Life After a Painful Divorce

By

Jonathan K. Sanders

Published by

Queen V Publishing
Dayton, Ohio
QueenVPublishing.net

Published by

Queen V Publishing
Dayton, Ohio
QueenVPublishing.net
Info@PenoftheWriter.com

Copyright © 2009 by Jonathan K. Sanders

All rights reserved. No part of this book may be reproduced or transmitted in any form or by any means, electronic or mechanical, without prior written consent of the Publisher, except for the inclusion of brief quotes in a review.

All Scripture quotations—unless otherwise indicated—are taken from the King James Version of the Holy Bible.

Scripture quotations marked NKJV are taken from the Holy Bible, New King James Version. Copyright 1982 by Thomas Nelson, Inc. Used by permission. All rights reserved.

Scripture quotations marked NLT are taken from the Holy Bible, New Living Translation. Copyright 1996, 2004. Used by permission of Tyndale House Publishers, Inc., Wheaton, IL 60189. All rights reserved.

Scripture quotations marked NASB are taken from the New American Standard Bible (registered mark). Copyright 1960, 1962, 1963, 1968, 1971, 1972, 1973, 1975, 1977, 1995 by The Lockman Foundation. Used by permission.

Library of Congress Control Number: 2009907954

ISBN-13: 978-0-9817436-6-0

Cover design by Candace K

Printed in the United States of America

Dedication

This book is dedicated to anyone who has survived a divorce, knows a survivor of divorce or wants to divorce proof their marriage.

Acknowledgements

To those who influenced me the most, I offer sincere gratitude:

Bishop Fred and Esther Sanders—my loving parents. You taught me commitment and persistence. The words you spoke and continue to speak in my spirit remind me that this is just the beginning.

My wonderful sons—Jonathan and Joshua. You bring me joy. The world awaits you, soldiers.

Table of Contents

Introduction 1
Chapter 1
   Issues with Divorce in the Church 3
      Can I Marry Again? 4
Chapter 2
   Warning 6
      The Signs Before a Painful Divorce 6
      Served and Being Served 7
      True Feelings Revealed 7
Chapter 3
   Church Criticism & Family Reaction 9
      How Your Family Really Felt 9
      Who Made You My Judge? 11
      Preaching Under Pressure 12
Chapter 4
   Feelings 14
      Who's to Blame? 14
      False Evidence Appearing Real 16
      Bad Habits Coming Back 18
      How Long Will I Feel Like This? 21
Chapter 5
   Money, Money, Money...MONEY! 22
      Should You Benefit from the Divorce If You Caused It? 23
Chapter 6
   What About the Children? 30
      Children Caught in the Shuffle 30
      It's All About the Children, Right? 31
      A Change of Religion 32

Chapter 7
Social Separation 34
Mob Mentality 34
My Mood is Different 34
Environment is Everything 35
Creating New Surroundings 35

Chapter 8
The Other Sex 38
Never See Women the Same 38
Where There is Admire There is Desire 40
Sex is the Last Resort for a Companion 42

Chapter 9
Rated R 46
Marriage is Honorable 47
A Human Magnet 48
Masturbation 49

Chapter 10
Should I Look For Another or Stay By Myself? 50
They That Wait Upon the Lord 52
Can I Divorce-Proof My Marriage? 55
Sometimes Opposites Attack 57
Flaws and All 58
Allergic to Kids 59
How Bad Do You Want It? 59
Cleanliness is Next to Godliness 60
Commitment 61

Chapter 11
Delivered From Divorce 64
The Transition 64
Who's Next? 65
The Bounce-Back Factor 68

End Notes 71
About Jonathan K. Sanders 72

Introduction

You've heard "what doesn't kill you makes you stronger," but what about the thing that makes you sick as hell? Like coughing up divorce in conversations, sneezing divorce every time you are offended or bleeding divorce when someone steps on your toes. That's my story. After celebrating thirteen years of marriage and being blessed with two sons, divorce became my reality.

Statistics indicate that forty to sixty percent of all marriages will end in divorce. Whether you choose to accept it, the fact remains: divorce is destroying families worldwide. Many of my friends—in and out of the church—progressed after divorce, while others digressed by turning to alcohol, drugs, sex and more. Some chose to give up on love all together or tried an alternative lifestyle. Some of my divorced female friends have sworn to never trust a man again. They consider all men dogs or a means to get their bills paid. Some of my divorced male counterparts look to women as objects of sexual gratification or gold diggers trying to take them for every dime.

My purpose for this book is not to place blame, paint a picture of perfection or gain sympathy. I will not provide details that may shed a negative light on my ex-wife. I will however, share how the divorce affected me. I will impart spiritual and practical wisdoms that helped me transition from hurt to healing. I fought through tears, mood swings, loss of appetite and public embarrassment.

I overcame discouragement and loneliness. I discovered my true friends.

This book is not only for my brothers and sisters in the Lord, but for those who may not profess the Christian life as well. My prayer is that you will see the light of God's love in spite of what you have experienced.

Divorce doesn't have to be the end, but rather a new beginning that awaits you. Know that you still have so much to live for. As one who has endured the process of maturation, I encourage you to walk in confidence. Hold your head high because your future promises to be great. And by all means, don't give up on love because there is *Life After a Painful Divorce*.

In His love,

Jonathan K. Sanders

Chapter 1
Issues with Divorce in the Church

Divorce is a sensitive topic and one of the most controversial subjects in the church. Albeit common —the divorce rate among Christians exceeds the national average—few pastors delve into it. Some Christians believe that if you've been divorced, God won't forgive you. And remarriage? That takes on a whole other spin on sin.

The Bible states that only one sin is exempt from His redemptive power.

> *Wherefore I say unto you, All manner of sin and blasphemy shall be forgiven unto men: but the blasphemy [against] the [Holy] Ghost shall not be forgiven unto men.*
> Matthew 12:31

Christians often misinterpret the following verse:

> *"For I hate divorce," says the Lord, the God of Israel, "and him who covers his garment with wrong," says the Lord of hosts. "So take heed to your spirit that you do not deal treacherously."*
> Malachi 2:16 NASB

Can I Marry Again?

Many Christians believe that you cannot marry again once you've been divorced. Please know that the Bible doesn't say that, but man's traditions do. If your sins are forgiven by the grace of God, why would divorce be excluded? If a man can be forgiven of robbery or rape; if a woman can be forgiven for an abortion, then why can't you be forgiven for a failed marriage?

You see, it's easy for a person—on the outside looking in—to tell you to stay in your marriage. As stated in Amos 3:3, "How can two walk together expect they be agreed?" What father wants his daughter married to a man who beats her? What woman wants to be married to an unfaithful man who has infected her with a sexually-transmitted disease. God is not the author of confusion.

They believe that divorce is unforgivable in the eyes of God. The accused walk around as if they are forever tainted with a mark of sin. The accuser ignores the hurt and often inflicts more pain with insensitive comments.

I am not a proponent of divorce. I prefer that couples fight to maintain the holy institution of marriage. I learned the hard way that no matter how much you want a relationship to work, it will not survive if your spouse wants out of the marriage.

If you learn only one thing from this book, know that divorce hurts men too! Men have been trained to be tough and hardcore so we often suffer in silence. Although we appear strong, masked pain resonates deep inside.

My being a preacher did not stop me from becoming a divorce statistic. Current data indicates that more than half of all marriages will end in divorce. Christian marriages have an even higher divorce rate estimated at almost 60%. Why? Because we go into marriage as broken vessels expecting our mates to fill the cracks and crevices. We don't prepare ourselves for oneness because we believe that being Christians is enough. Our churches do not provide effective marriage ministries to impart biblical and practical techniques nor create an environment to share in confidence without reprise or retaliation. So we hide marital strife to shun the shame and appearance of inadequacy. As for professional counseling? In certain communities, counseling is deemed an option only for the insane.

Second marriages fail at 65% due in part to the spouses coming to the relationship with unresolved issues from the first marriage. The dynamics of stepfamilies when children —and yes, adult children—are involved has a major impact on second marriages. Following the trend, as the number of repeat marriages rise, the divorce rate climbs as well. Third marriages have a high incidence of divorce at almost 75%.

African-American couples divorce at a rate of 70%; second only to that of entertainers and professional athletes (80%).

Your newlywed-acting friends who have been married for years may shock you one day with the disturbing news that their once beautiful and secure marriage is headed for divorce court.

You can deny it, ignore it or even say that divorce will never happen to you. The fact remains: divorce is destroying families worldwide.

Chapter 2
Warning

<u>The Signs Before a Painful Divorce</u>

The temperature in the house has changed. No welcome-home kiss to greet you. The cute little things your spouse has always done now aggravate you. Innocent requests escalate to intense arguments. Affirming words and complements have transformed into accusations and assaults. All that's reminiscent of those special love trinkets is an occasional peace offering. Conversations about bills and the children have replaced pillow talk. A virtual solid-steel wall has been erected in your bed or worse yet, you sleep in separate rooms.

For some, the atmospheric pressure has such a dramatic change that recognizing the tornado-like climate shift is easy. While for others, the gradual ozone depletion goes unnoticed until the rising tsunami waters bring great floods and devastation. Each relationship—and each person within the relationship—is different. One disgruntled spouse may have his/her mate come home to a house void of family and furniture, while another may embody a landlord-to-tenant mentality and give a thirty-day notice to vacate the premises. While you're out buying an offertory outfit to apologize for last night's argument, your mate is seated at the desk of a high-powered attorney.

Served and Being Served

Serving papers can be joyous or distressing depending upon where you stand in the process: the server or the servee. Like signing mortgage documents for your first home or getting a letter from your doctor indicating that you have terminal cancer with six months left to live.

How is it that a couple can have deep feelings for each other, but once the divorce is final, all that love is flushed down the toilet? The new behavior is like the waste treatment facility that churns the raw sewage. Did love ever abide in the union? The depth of your relationship and integrity as a person can be measured by how you treat and respond to your soon-to-be ex.

True Feelings Revealed

The first feeling that overtook me was failure. I used my parents' marriage as a measuring stick of marital success. My parents have been married for over forty years and I planned for my marriage to at least match their longevity.

It's a beautiful thing to go to a couple's home and see pictures of them dating several decades back. Naming your grandchildren and great grandchildren is a privilege. Of course they've had troubles, but love is the glue that keeps them together. And though they don't look anything like they did years ago, their love has gotten stronger.

Failure told me, "You will never reach that goal so don't even try. Even if you do remarry, medical science only gives you about seventy-one years of life. By the time you meet, date and marry, you'll do good to see twenty years of marital strife — I mean bliss."

When I stood up to fear and resolved the dissolution of my goal, only then was I able to look in the mirror and admit that some things are not meant to be.

Chapter 3
Church Criticism & Family Reaction

What are they going to say? How are they going to look at me? Am I a failure in their eyes? Will they think it's my fault? Am I still respected in the church or should I resign my position?

Although you may never verbalize these questions, they will cross your mind. Have you ever said, "I don't care what people think about me," but you knew that to be untrue?" Even Jesus spoke out of concern for what people thought of Him.

> *When Jesus came into the coasts of Caesarea Philippi, He asked His disciples, saying, "Who do men say that I, the Son of Man, am?"*
> Matthew 16:13

Be honest. We all care, but on different levels. We care about the opinions of people who care about us. For those with whom we don't have much interaction, not so much.

How Your Family Really Felt

The response from family can help or hinder your healing. A son needs to be reaffirmed by his mother as does a daughter by her father. The validation renews confidence and develops a foundation for restoration. No woman wants to hear her father say, "You didn't treat him right. You should have cooked and cleaned instead of working overtime. You talk back too much. No wonder you're divorced. This mess is your fault!" Don't misunderstand me; both spouses have a role in the demise of the marriage, but save the "constructive criticism" for later.

Being overwhelmed with failure is one thing, but the scolding of a parent can devastate a wounded soul beyond repair. Other than the leading of the Lord, they have been a voice of reason.

Want to know which of your siblings liked your spouse and who hated the fact that your mate consumed oxygen? The same sister who was a bridesmaid and smiled in your face on your wedding day may give you a piece of her mind before the dust settles on your divorce decree.

"I never liked him for you in the first place," "You could have done better than her," or "I probably should have told you this earlier, but while you were dating..." This purge of guilt is unfair to the newly divorced. To bombard a sibling with "could have; would have; should have" does nothing but further substantiate low self-esteem and bad judge of character. Why is it that everyone else saw the pending doom and you missed it? The clairvoyant could have kept you from being a shriveled fragment of life in the corner. Oh, now you want to be a psychic!

Who Made You My Judge?

> *Judge not, that ye be not judged.*
> Matthew 7:1

Ah, the church: the place of refuge and strength; the house of healing and restoration; the advocate for openness and transparency. The church: filled with judgmental, accusatory, fault-finding folks who charge you guilty and sentence you to life without the possibility of parole. The church: the breeding ground for hypocrites and haters; a place where people wear the mask of perfection and seventh-heaven holiness.

None of us are perfect, but striving to be perfected. As quiet as it's kept, we have all messed up and disappointed the Lord.

> *For all have sinned, and come short of the glory of God.*
> Romans 3:23

Many saints sing, preach, shout and worship with a bleeding heart because of divorce or other life crisis. How can the church accept and forgive drug use, fornication and homosexuality, yet shun those who have been divorced? It's the most hypocritical spirit operating in church today. Few ministries have programs that address needs specific to the divorced, albeit the largest growing population in the congregation. They have programs for children, youth, men and women; substance abuse programs; community outreach ministries and more. But where do broken hearts go: the church, the psychiatrist or the club?

Preaching Under Pressure

I have preached across the world and ministered to thousands while bleeding internally from hurt and failure. If it had not been for the Spirit of God, I don't see how I could have made it. Church leaders are expected to have power and experience, but those attributes come after tribulation.

I remember saying that I wished the churches would give me a break but the calls doubled and I didn't seem to have time to heal. I boarded planes and checked in and out of hotel rooms while thinking, *How can I help others when I can't help myself?* I didn't feel comfortable sharing with other preachers since they can also be judgmental.

I had hoped to receive spiritual solace from my father, but he simply said, "You're not the first and you certainly won't be the last."

"Wow," was all I could say. A brother can't get holy oil, laying on of hands or prophecy?

As an ex-marine, the phrase, "only the strong survive," played in my mind. I used to sit in the church office before ministering. While the anointed praise and worship went forth in the sanctuary, the fear of failing the people —and more importantly God—tormented me. But by the time my hand touched the microphone, my spirit lifted and the Scripture spoke to my heart.

> *And not only so, but we glory in tribulations also: knowing that tribulation worketh patience; and patience, experience; and experience, hope.*
>
> Romans 5:3-4

> *Not by might, nor by power, but by My Spirit, saith the Lord of hosts.*
>
> Zechariah 4:6

Once I realized that this situation was not about me and that I had people counting on me—my parents, children and peers—I was able to finish the task.

I commend my church family. They never treated me differently and I count that a blessing. Although at times, it appeared that some stood with baited breath to see if I would crumble under pressure.

"Bend, don't break."

Chapter 4
Feelings

I once said that divorce is like being cut in half while still alive. The termination of a marriage has also been compared to ripping a sheet of paper and then trying to put it back together like new. Impossible. Jagged edges, small tears and unseen fragments do not allow for a simple paste or tape fix. Beyond the severance of ties, allocation of assets and establishment of visitation, insomnia, loss of appetite, mood swings and depression complicate the healing process. With that said, unless you've experienced the pains of divorce, you'll never fully understand its impact.

Who's to Blame?

The who's-to-blame song will play in your mind until you decide to stop the music. Human nature seeks to find the source of the problem and more often than not, we start from the outside. It is easy to blame the ex for the demise of the relationship, however in so doing, your flaws go uncorrected. Just like "it takes two to make a thing go right," it also takes two to make a thing go wrong.

Even if the influence of a third party led to the divorce, the outcome inevitably falls upon the two spouses. The couple stood before God and man when they vowed to "forsake all others."

Life After a Painful Divorce

I was in my late thirties at the time of my divorce. I believed that I was a well-versed, educated man. Through this process, I learned a lot about myself, my ex and marriage as a whole. I have an intimate understanding of the statement "you can learn as much from success as you can failure."

Only a mature person can accept the part they played in the ruin of a marriage. Without introspection, ignoring your contribution will spew over into your next relationship, wreaking havoc. And after several rounds of defeat, you may find yourself blaming everyone of the opposite sex. Look in the mirror and work through it. The process will not be easy, but what's the worse that can happen? You identify some shortcomings and then commit to improve and reinvent yourself.

Johari's Window[1]—created by Joseph Luft and Harry Ingham—helps individuals develop better relationships through improved interpersonal-communication skills. The window identifies four components—or panes—of awareness:

1. Things others know about me that I know (arena)
2. Things others know about me that I don't know (blind spot)
3. Things that others or I don't know about me (unknown)
4. Things I know about me that no one else knows (façade)

Create a checklist of pros and cons. Ask family and friends to describe you in four words: two positive and two not-so positive. Get a feel for who you are from the perspective of others. To get a true feel for their opinion, ask them to mail responses to you for anonymity. Tally the results and compare your adjectives with theirs.

False Evidence Appearing Real

Fear. **F**alse **E**vidence **A**ppearing **R**eal. Why do I feel like a failure, when I did not even want the divorce? Meeting after meeting with lawyers, real-estate agents, family mediators and bank advisors wore on me, but nothing burdened me more than the custody battle for my children. To have the fate of my children determined by a judge gripped me with fear.

I am a participatory father. I get involved and stay involved in my children's activities. In addition to instructing them on the ways of God, I help with homework, counsel them about women—as best I can—and hang out with them. We ride bikes, play basketball and frequent the local game room. I still hold the title as Air Hockey King.

I think that a father should spend quality time with his children. Guidance and impartation of wisdom don't happen by telepathy, and fulfilling financial obligations isn't enough to nurture responsible adults. Sadly, I didn't get a lot of time with my father. He preached around the world, ministered to thousands; but never attended one of my basketball games or tossed a ball in the yard. With eight children, it was understandable that he had to do what was necessary to support his family. I never held that against him, but I vowed to be active in my children's lives.

I have flown around the world and experienced numerous holding patterns. Due to inclement weather, arriving too soon or problems on the ground, the air traffic controller directed the pilot to circle the airport until the matter was resolved. The delay ripples into more delays, missed connecting flights and frustrated passengers who have no control over the situation. Waiting for the outcome of the divorce proceedings put me into a holding pattern and consumed my every thought. My life came to a dead stop. I could not function. I could not focus. What if the magistrate decides that my boys will get better care from their mother? When will I get to see them? How will that affect our relationship? The sermons that I preached to encourage others, I had to draw upon for my own peace of mind.

"No matter what you're going through, God has your back. He promised that He'd never leave or forsake you so stand in the midst of your storm, grab your anchor and hold on. He's got you covered."

Even the Scripture on my business cards boasted about my faith in Him.

> *What shall we then say to these things? If God be for us, who can be against us?*
> Romans 8:31

After months of waiting, I tried to reason with God and call in a favor.

"Lord, You are the potter and I am the clay. You are the blacksmith and I am the precious metal. You are the creator and I am the creation. I know that You have my best interest at heart, but Lord, this one is too much. I can't take anymore. I have done what You asked and I need You to come through for me right now."

Well, the Lord called my bluff. Not being able to go one more day, turned into holding on a few more weeks and then months. He knew that I would not walk out on my children or Him and more importantly, He knew that I needed a little more time in the purifying fire.

Through that agonizing wait, I learned that when I felt most alone, God was working it out for my good. Like the air traffic controller, He saw things that I couldn't. Despite the minor inconvenience, He steered me clear of turbulence and taught me how to trust Him in the midst of turmoil.

> *Unless the Lord had been my help, my soul had almost dwelt in silence when I said my foot slippeth, Thy mercy, oh Lord, held me up.*
>
> Psalm 94:17-18

Bad Habits Coming Back

Divorce can cause you to develop productive coping mechanisms or revert to bad habits. I know people who did a self-inventory, reinvented themselves and live a great life. I also have friends—both in and out of the church—who turned to alcohol, drugs or sex in an effort to comfort the hurt. Several decided to give up on heterosexual love and embarked on a gay lifestyle. Some of my female friends classify men as dogs and a means to get bills paid. While my male buddies, look at women as objects of sexual gratification or gold-digging hustlers.

When you are emotionally, mentally and financially spent, your defense is down. You become a vulnerable target open to anything that pacifies you. Destructive behaviors and bad habits that you conquered years ago may reappear seven times stronger.

Life After a Painful Divorce

Divorce deflates a man's self-esteem like a hot air balloon with a faulty burner. Getting a man to admit that is next to impossible, but believe me, it's true. Men internalize the rejection and use it to measure worth. To boost the perceived worthlessness, many men turn to women. Once the word is out that a new bachelor is "on the market," opportunities are presented at the mall, church and work. What one woman tossed aside, many sisters are willing to pick up, dust off and take home. Sir, with your ego at zero, can you handle the temptation? Get to the place where you encourage yourself. Don't pacify; mortify the flesh.

> *So put to death the sinful, earthly things lurking within you. Have nothing to do with sexual sin, impurity, lust and shameful desires. Don't be greedy for the good things of this life, for that is idolatry.*
>
> Colossians 3:5 NLT

What about the wife who endured years of verbal abuse and left the marriage feeling ugly? Sure the new lipstick makes her feel a little better about herself, but it's the absence of negative energy that carries the real power.

Pygmalion effect[2] is a means of asserting psychological control to influence a person's behavior. The tool can be used to ignite passion or diffuse aggression. If you repeatedly tell someone that they will never amount to anything, self-perception embodies those words and materializes in their actions. If you hear a lie enough times, you begin to believe it.

> *For as he thinketh in his heart, so [is] he: Eat and drink, saith he to thee; but his heart [is] not with thee.*
>
> Proverbs 23:7

Be Careful

Be careful of your thoughts,
for your thoughts become your words.
Be careful of your words,
for your words become your actions.
Be careful of your actions,
for your actions become your habits.
Be careful of your habits,
for your habits become your character.
Be careful of your character,
for your character becomes your destiny.
—Author unknown

To fight off the psychological fiery darts of the enemy, master encouraging yourself. Look in the mirror, flash that great smile, say, "I have worth. I am attractive. I deserve the best God has for me." While you're flattering you, meditate on His Word.

> *And the Lord shall make thee the head, and not the tail; and thou shalt be above only, and thou shalt not be beneath; if that thou hearken unto the commandments of the Lord thy God, which I command thee this day, to observe and to do [them].*
>
> Deuteronomy 28:13

> *These things I have spoken unto you, that in Me ye must have peace. In the world ye will have tribulation; but be of good cheer; I have overcome the world.*
>
> John 16:33

I have observed a divorcee jump into a new relationship with the ink still wet on the divorce decree. Don't be fooled into believing that a new companion is the solution. You must be totally healed and restored if you ever expect to have a fulfilled relationship. Otherwise, you'll be like a horse on a merry-go-round—going around in circles from one failed relationship to the next.

How Long Will I Feel Like This?

Experts have indicated that the grieving process takes a minimum of two years. That period allows the griever to experience holidays, birthdays and other memorable dates. Since divorce is a type of death, don't expect an overnight remedy. The healing process will take time and effort.

I encourage you to invest in your recovery: obtain the services of a professional counselor, take a vacation, get a massage or read a good book. Do something that refreshes you toward healing.

Chapter 5
Money, Money, Money...MONEY!

How will I pay my bills? Will I lose my car, house, everything I have accumulated during the marriage?

On the surface, two incomes should equal more money, but that may not always be the case. Possibly due to a lack of trust or the inability to relinquish control, many couples do not combine incomes. I know couples who have never seen each other's pay stub. Amazing.

Because of this, that is why you can make it with one or two incomes. It's all about how you have handle your finances throughout your entire life, not while just married. That's why some people who have never been married still own a home, car or business. God has destined you to be blessed. That blessing is not connected to a marriage contract.

> *But my God shall supply all your need according to His riches in glory by Christ Jesus.*
> Philippians 4:19

If you want to get to the heart of a person's character, see how they act when it comes to money—in abundance and lack. I have heard of divorcing couples who fabricate untruths to get over financially. The worse is when a man dodges the responsibility of caring for his children.

Is it true that women get the bigger piece of the pie financially or is it simply a myth? Should one get more

Life After a Painful Divorce

than the other solely based on gender? Of course men say, "No." Almost every woman I know says "yes," despite the fact that many women make comparable salaries with respect to men. Or should the most money go to the one who got the short end of the stick. For example, the man who runs off with his mistress and leaves his family, or the woman who skips town with her boss. Why should one be rewarded with the fruits of marriage—house, car, spousal support—when they cut down the family tree?

Should You Benefit from the Divorce If You Caused It?

I applaud individuals who bow out gracefully because of indiscretions. Some men know they messed up, slept around and were physically abusive. But the sign of a bad man gone good, is when he decides to release his wife—without a fight—because he's unable to remain faithful, cannot stop the abuse or realized that he's not the marrying type. Some women abandon their family for a new man who can "put it down," yet still want spousal support, the car and the kitchen sink. Is the best reality a good lawyer or just placing it in God's hand? Both. Don't be a fool and don't be super spiritual.

When I learned how much I had to pay to settle my divorce, I felt like I had been punched in the throat by a heavy-weight champion: speechless, breathless, dazed and confused. I wanted to stay in our house, while she wanted to sell it. The disparity tortured me. I loved our home. The neighborhood—with its mature trees, manicured landscapes and filled with the laughter of children—reminded me of a sunny California town. I knew most of the neighbors by first name and it was in walking distance from the kids' elementary school. Tears welled in my eyes when the real-estate agent put the "For Sale" sign in the front yard.

As I worked on the lawn or washed my car, my neighbors inquired, "Where are you moving to?" Embarrassed, I tactfully found a way to change the subject.

Oh, but thank God for legal representation with the experiential foresight to see what I could not. My lawyer advised that to maintain stability for the children, I should buy my wife out and stay in the home. I agreed. As a result, it minimized disruption to my boys' routine by introducing them to only one new environment—their mother's residence.

But right after that, I was faced with child support which would have been no problem because I was raised by a father to always take care or your kids. But when the arguments came and I was told, "I'll do whatever I want with your money," I sought advice from my lawyer. I knew I wanted joint custody anyway because I could never deal with just getting my boys on the weekends. That was when I was told by my lawyer that I needed to pursue joint custody. That would give me a total of two weeks a month with my boys. I prayed to God because I love my kids and this option would be the ultimate blessing! I even fasted the day of court for favor with the magistrate. Prayer answers things. Not only was joint custody awarded, I was named the custodial parent: the boys' primary home was at my residence. I danced so much that I could have taken James Brown's crown! Despite a system that often labels men as "deadbeat dads who don't care about their children," God favored my petition.

Life After a Painful Divorce

The boys expressed excitement too. They had love for both parents and did not want to solely be at either parent's house. I tell my fellow brethren that kids are often placed with their mothers because most fathers do not fight for custody. Many men don't want to spend the time with their children or the money which you will have to do one or the other. According to the National Center for Health Statistics, the courts side with women ninety percent of the time in custody battles. Custody battles seem to be hardest on African-American fathers probably because of the combination of gender and racial discrimination. But thank God men are waking up, forming organizations like the Fatherhood Educational Institute and the website DadsRights.com. Men, take your rightful place. Let's let the world see that good Black fathers exist.

The situation gets much stickier when you have a relationship and your new companion doesn't want your kids around. I know too many examples to name. I'm shocked how someone can choose a lover or spouse over their own children! I've even known some men to move in with a woman who has kids but his kids are not welcomed. Ridiculous! Just imagine how the children feel? Sometimes it's best to wait if you have small children instead of forcing someone on your kids. In my studies, children issues are one of the main reasons couple's divorce. Clashes erupt between your kids and their kids. Most children want to see their biological parents together, but when they mature they understand differently. I've personally watched my sons change over the past few years. At first, they never said anything about a woman, but as teenagers, they often ask, "Where are the ladies, Dad?" It's quite amusing now that I think about it.

Don't be so hard up for companionship that it will destroy the trunk of the family tree.

I'm excited to know the pendulum has swung in the favor of the women. They have imported cars, their own house, money, ministry and even their own businesses. Hey we even had a woman presidential candidate on the ballot! Female pastors, sheriffs, mayors, and the list continues. A new type of woman is on the forefront and this brings great excitement to real men who are not inferior. The new type of woman that I'm seeing is an absolute breath of fresh air to society. However where there's the new, the old is still somewhere hanging around. Despite this fast trend that's sweeping across the world there are still some women who have the old mentality that they can only receive and never give. It's not unusual for a woman to ask the man out, pay for the movie, and dinner! This may sound contrary to some women but if you ask him out, shouldn't you cover the cost? Women that receive and do not give back into the relationship nothing but time and conversation will find it hard to get a good man. Although God created men to be givers and women receivers, can't a brother get a home-cooked meal, a card or a gift just to know he's special and appreciated?

It's a major turnoff when I meet a woman who off the back carries the aroma of just being a taker. This is why I believe so many men at times are apprehensive about certain relationships. Some men will spoil you to death: fly you around the country on an all inclusive trip; buy you jewelry, clothes and even support your children financially in the absence of their dead-beat daddy! One of my brothers (I have four so stop guessing) took a young lady out on a date, and before dinner was over she

Life After a Painful Divorce

asked if she could order food to go for her children. He was cool with it and said okay. Over their next three dates, she repeated her take-home order. On the fourth date, he told her that her actions were crass. And would you believe she had the nerve to get an attitude? Needless to say, the dating ceased.

A woman with a 720 FICO score is far more attractive to me than long hair and French-tip nails. The hair may be weaved, the tips fake, but a good credit rating cannot be counterfeited! We brothers don't mind bringing the table and chairs, just help us put something on it! When I see a sister that has her own it is one of the most elegant things I've ever seen. So many women use the excuse for where they are by saying that they don't have a man, they have kids and no child support or bad credit is culprit. Yet these same women are the ones spending all their money on hair care products, clothes and going out to eat three times a week with their girlfriends. So tell me who's to blame for the page they are on in their lives?

Competition is high among women, which has caused many to wear their wealth on their backs. And despite the insurmountable bills that keep piling up, they go to church, hucking and bucking, breaking fingernails, losing ponytails, saying "Lord, make a way." He made a way with an income-earning job, but many have cursed themselves with bad decisions which eventually become bad habits.

Being divorced may cost you lots of money. When you are on the financial rebound and have finally landed on your feet, your money mentality will greatly improve. I cried on how much my divorced cost me, but I dried my eyes quickly because I had a father who taught me from a young age how to handle money and not let money handle me. He pushed me to get my first job as a grocery-store bagger at twelve. At fifteen years old, I worked at McDonald's. When I showed him my first check—expecting a handshake, full smile and congratulations—he deducted fifty dollars and called it my monthly rent payment. What in the world? A teenager with a mortgage? My nostrils flared and sweat beaded on my forehead (I knew better than to verbally challenge my father, but I couldn't control the nonverbal rage). Today I realize that he taught me principles of financial stewardship that will benefit me throughout life.

I compel anyone coming out of divorce to stand on your own feet. Don't run to your parents or friends who will try to rescue you. Walk the burning embers of financial restoration; bring forth pure fruit; take pride in your accomplishment. If you have to leave a four-bedroom home with a two-car garage and start with a one-bedroom apartment in the hood, at least your name will be on the lease. I see people who just keep company with others that will feed into their needs instead of pushing them to take the long, but sure way.

I will admit that when I first got divorced, I was caught up in buying things to mask my pain such as clothes, lavish vacations, expensive restaurants, jewelry and the like. I never realized how buying is connected to how you feel inside. I noticed when I bought things I would say this is going to help me get over the divorce. How silly was I? What does a white-gold ring or a $500 suit have to do with your inner mental healing? Not a thing. So many of my peers have been operating on this level for years and still are without financial maturity ever kicking in! They have twenty pairs of gators, three or four cars with high payments, $25,000 in jewelry and clothes like a department store, all to mask how they really feel inside. Happiness is not having what you want but wanting what you have.

Chapter 6
What About the Children?

<u>Children Caught in the Shuffle</u>

I have never experienced the pain of a severed limb, but a severed heart; excruciating. The worse feeling I have endured was to see the pain in my children's eyes. Unlike a drowning child, my boys never cried out for help but I read their eyes: hurt, afraid, confused. The pain pierced deep, so I asked my then wife to prolong filing the divorce.

She emphatically said, "No! I want out! Just tell the boys that we both want this."

"That's a lie." I argued. "I don't want this divorce, you do!" My head and heart were open to work on the marriage and I knew God's stance on it. So where do I go?

Initially, I refused to let go. In doing so, I said within myself, *I'm going to hold you against your will and make you be with me.* In some states, that's kidnapping. Love should captivate, not capture.

Let's say that your car has been jacked by an armed assailant. You drive your fingernails into the rear bumper unwilling to let this jerk speed away with what you worked so hard to obtain. He careens down an alley at sixty miles-per-hour dragging you through potholes and broken bottles. What began as a refusal to give up your car now jeopardizes your life. Let go, file a claim with your insurance company and get another car.

When you let go, you save yourself unnecessary pain and heartache. Forgiveness. Don't disrespect yourself or God by thinking that because this person left you, your life is over. God didn't design you to stalk—spying through binoculars or calling twenty times an hour from a blocked number. In letting go, you open yourself to the positive energy that can connect you with someone better. Love can be better the second time around.

I've heard horror stories about children of divorced parents who went buck wild. To numb the pain or in a desperate attempt for attention, they delve into sex, drugs, truancy, even suicide. I had invested much time and love into developing my boys into men, yet I feared the worse.

Refusing to lie to my boys, I stated my objection on numerous occasions which led to many arguments. When the divorce was inevitable, I had a heart-to-heart chat with my boys who were then ten and eleven years old.

I explained that their mother and I loved them. In an effort to minimize their guilt, I reiterated that the divorce was not their fault. I compelled them to not harbor resentment.

"Your mother is not a bad person however she believes that this choice is in her best interest."

A major factor in their resilience was that my then wife and I both loved them through the transition. We committed to spending quality and quantity time with them. We reassured them of our love both in word and deed.

It's All About the Children, Right?

"Your request for joint custody will be denied." The agonizing words of her attorney reverberated through me.

Once the shock wave subsided, anguish settled. What was her motive for denying me time with my boys? I have witnessed the chaos caused on so many children—especially boys—whose fathers were absent.

"Satan, not my boys!"

Up to that point, I had been accommodating and amicable, but when the furnace was ignited, I turned up the heat. I showed up at my attorney's office for an unscheduled meeting.

"Whatever it takes to make this happen, make it happen. I am not a child-support-pay-check daddy. I'm a quality-time daddy." I placed a wad of money on his desk. "I'm ready for the fight of my life. They need me in their lives and I need them in mine."

My attorney said, "Jonathan, it can get expensive. You will have to hire a private lawyer to represent them solely. They may even have to take the stand in court and state where they want to live."

I encouraged my sons to be honest with the magistrate. I refused to put undue pressure on them and expressed that I supported whatever decision they made.

"We want to be with both you and Mommy."

When their mother heard what they were going to say, she backed down. The boys did not have to endure questioning and I won guardianship as the custodial parent. Hallelujah!

A Change of Religion

I breathed relief and celebrated for eight minutes and then she told the boys that she had changed religion and was a member of the Nation of Islam. After being a Christian for thirteen years and accepting her calling as a minister, she migrated to the Muslim faith. What in the world? For a brief moment, I wondered if she was ever saved. But seeing as how I am a ways off from perfection, I decided not to be judgmental.

When they returned from a visit with their mother, the boys told me that they were no longer allowed to eat pork. She told them that swine was not good for them and she would not be buying or preparing it. I don't mind a little pork on my fork, so that rule didn't transfer to my house.

The boys bombarded me with questions about this new religion. They grew up in Christianity and the contradicting values and beliefs confused them—and me. How can you walk with God faithfully for thirteen years and then change gods because of divorce? What did Jesus do to turn her away from Him?

As clearly as the words are printed on this page, God spoke to me. He told me that I must not fuss or argue with her, but simply pray for the sister.

"Sir, yes Sir!"

Chapter 7
Social Separation

Divorce can make you retreat from or advance toward socialization. You may avoid certain people or groups you once cherished while clinging to new—seemingly incompatible—folks. The shift is a matter of trust. Weddings and funerals bring out the real person. I'm adding divorce to that list.

Mob Mentality

Some people will step back from you as if you had a deep, raspy cough during a flu pandemic and you didn't bother to cover your mouth. These spectators stand on the sidelines waiting to see the outcome of the game: will you fold under the pressure or will you come out on top?

While some run away from you, a plethora of others run toward you. They come bringing gifts of unsolicited advice, invitations to pity parties and a list of unmarried friends looking to get hitched. You didn't ask for a cheerleading squad when an occasional, "Are you okay?" would suffice.

My Mood is Different

The bombardment of negativity from the ex—or others in disbelief of the divorce—can lead to self-induced isolation. It's easier to mope alone than the continuous recitation of the gory details.

On the other hand, introspection can reveal things about yourself that you would rather not believe, so you seek solace from strangers for validation. Misery loves company.

Environment is Everything

To maneuver through the alternating moods, I learned the power of navigation. Navigation is influence. Either you influence your environment or it influences you.

I grew up in the projects of Harlem with gangs, guns and prostitution. A standard fixture in the community was a plastered heroin user slumped in the gutter. I didn't know good neighborhoods existed. Even the ones on TV were like something out of a fairytale. But as my dad's ministry grew we moved to Jamaica, Queens. The ten of us—Mom, Dad, five boys, three girls—lived in a house rather than a three-bedroom apartment. I thought the garage in the back was somebody else's house! It was almost too real to believe that this house was now our home. From the pit to the palace. Hallelujah!

Stay away from people who try to keep your conversation in the past. If you dwell on the past, that's where you'll stay. Remember: we walk where we watch, so look to your future.

Creating New Surroundings

I challenge you to create a powerful environment which breeds success. Cleave to those who push you to your future. Find people who will support, encourage and challenge you. Once you've created your amen corner, take caution not to zap their energy with pathetic groveling. Don't use the divorce as an excuse for helplessness. No one wants to be around an adult who acts like a spoiled child—divorced or not. Don't take your supporters for granted. Express appreciation often.

When you see a person who is calm in the midst of a tumultuous storm, you witness someone who has adapted to the situation. If you live in an efficiency apartment, work a minimum-wage job but you're working toward home ownership, then surround yourself with people who have "arrived" where you're trying to get. If you want to be a millionaire, spend time with millionaires. If you want to be a doctor, network with doctors. If you want a home and financial stability… You get the point.

No one chooses your friends but you. Even God grants you liberty to pick your pals. Choice is a powerful privilege; use it wisely. Survey your relationship environment. Does it stimulate or suffocate you? If it's the latter, RUN!

A psychologist friend of mine said, "Show me your friends and I'll show you your future." If you have a negative environment absent of hope; darkness fills the future and you are in trouble. I make a conscience effort to have minimal interaction with bitter divorced people and the unhappily married. Try as you might, the conversation will migrate to "there is no such thing as a happy marriage" and "life is over after divorce." The truth of the matter is their situation does not have to be yours. If you allow their awful experience to ferment in your mind, a bag of what-ifs will filter into future relationships.

- What if she's acting nice until I marry her?
- What if he's only after my body?
- What if the interest is in what I have; not who I am?

We may never know the truth, but God does. A committed relationship with your heavenly Father can help you stay focused on His will and not your own. Just as a close friend has your back, He has a way of warning you of pending danger. Will you listen or will that woman's beauty or that man's physique drown out His voice?

Chapter 8
The Other Sex

<u>Never See Women the Same</u>

After the divorce, I looked at women differently. My experience with one woman angered me so that it clouded my perspective toward all women (excluding my mother. She's the sweetest woman in the world. Don't laugh. That's my mother). Self-centered, manipulative and needy became my opinion. Regardless of how kind, intelligent, spiritual and beautiful, I perceived they had impure motives. Despite my twisted thinking, I tried not to disrespect or mistreat any woman. I ain't crazy. My mother wouldn't have it.

I opted for a disconnected connection with women. I gave them just enough of me to show interest but distanced myself emotionally. It only took a couple of outings for the façade to be revealed. Women looked at me like they had hit the chocolate lottery. Even though I told them that I was not ready for a relationship, they insisted that I would change my mind, once I got to know them. My advice: be considerate and forthright. If you intend to remain unattached and date several people, let each one of them know. I withdrew when the conversations got serious which led to arguments. I recognized my actions as a flaw in character and sought help. I went to the library to investigate. Guess what. I'm normal!

Life After a Painful Divorce

In my getting understanding, I learned that some men resort to nonproductive means. Some promise a lasting relationship knowing she's nothing more than a booty call. Others take deliberate steps to demoralize women as a form of payback to the ex-wife. What shocked me more than the antics of men was that women—desperate for the attention—allowed it. Tell me if any of these things sound familiar:

- Picking up the tab on a date that he initiated
- Running his errands
- Washing his clothes
- No public displays of affection (if you even go out together)
- And of course, spending quality time but only after midnight

This type of woman believes that if she keeps doing everything he wants, he will eventually become her man. That lie has to be the biggest one this side of the Mississippi River. Ladies, stop it! Love yourself more than you love being in a relationship.

I digress. I am not a psychologist but I have never met a man who was attracted to a woman he can treat like a doormat. His boo? Of course because she's at least feeding his ego and making him feel like he can have his way. Don't let men fool you, we love it. But when a man is picking a wife for life, or the queen of his dreams, he wants a woman who has a little backbone (just not bigger than his backbone). And there you have it. Man's best-kept secret: a doormat does not make a great wife.

I've heard elderly women say that a man is no match for a woman. After being out of the dating circle for over a decade, I learned that the "sistahs" had enough game to play in the NFL! Scandalous, manipulative, self centered.

At this quarter in life, I am less tolerant of foolishness. I am not labeling all women. I know women who embody the essence of virtue spoken of in Proverbs 31. While women can be the sweetest, kindest, most loving creations of God, others deserve an Oscar for the stellar performance of imitating a virtuous woman.

As I've said before, "Finding a good wife in a time like today is like finding a glass of ice water on the south side of hell!" Some women only look for men who have an influential or prestigious position such as a doctor, preacher, lawyer or any status that keeps her in the lime light. God help if she is only physically attracted without a desire for emotional connection. Flawless skin, enticing eyes, well-groomed, broad shoulders; none of these characteristics make the man. He can have all the looks yet be lazy, abusive, disrespectful and on the down low. You want him because he looks good and you look good with him? I think not.

Where There is Admire There is Desire

Some women are consumed with the title "girlfriend" or "wife." The moniker makes them feel whole, but they lose sight of the purpose of the relationship. I witnessed a woman manipulate a public display of affection—grabbing her man's hand—to mark her territory. She smiled, accentuated her sway and put him on display like he was a first-place medal at the Olympics. When a man feels he's been conquered like a city overthrown in a war, he will revolt.

When I deal with women, I ask, "Why am I here?" Is my role to wash her car, take out her trash, pay her bills, get her hair and nails done? In my experience, many women have the mentality that men should do all that and more. Let me clarify; I do not have a problem doing things for women, however reciprocity is critical in a relationship. If all she brings is long hair and stunning looks, I'm good. Chivalry is not dead, but no man wants to feel used like a sugar daddy.

A needy woman who gives nothing to sustain the relationship will run a man away. Since women can earn just as much money as men, doing a little something for a man on occasion, does not detract her femininity. When a man has a woman who will pick up the tab if he's low on funds, he has a jewel.

Women act differently when I'm in my Mercedes versus my '92 Camry. Guess which car I'm driving based on the following scenarios:

- The blinkers are flashing, I'm gesturing turn signals out the window, trying to make eye contact and women won't let me change lanes.
- Women smile, wave and call out to me.

A gold-digger is like a silent cancer and what's worse is that the church can be filled with them. Men are not looking for a wife in the church but rather in the kingdom. A church woman seeks a prophecy saying she will receive a husband who will pay her bills, while a kingdom woman understands the ways of a virtuous woman. She can manage her household and be a help to her husband. Kingdom women don't wait on a knight in shining armor—Armani custom-tailored suit—and white horse—Mercedes S Class—to rescue them from the dungeon of life. Kingdom women are employed homeowners who may have a business. Church women have the appearance of virtue as they jump and shout, dance and scream, but refuse to save for a home or get educated on investing.

Then they wonder why a brother from church dates a woman he met at the supermarket rather than a sister on the praise team. Don't be a damsel in financial distress; position yourself to receive His blessing.

Sex is the Last Resort for a Companion

Is sex overrated? You better believe it. Sex should be one of the last reasons for companionship. You can have a man who has bedroom skills that take you to the moon and back. But if he can't hold a steady job or is abusive—verbally or physically—is the great sex worth it?

Girlfriend may have the ability to drop it like it's hot and cause your pinky toes to curl up toward the heavens, but will her sex skills cause you to ignore her sixteen-year-old mentality? Doubtful.

Society has put sex and sexism at the top of the list. Music videos, tight jeans and low cut blouses are a part of life. I know women who have said that they won't even talk to a man with small feet and hands (Stop laughing. I'm telling the truth). Now what if that small-footed brother made $90,000 a year and owned a string of apartment complexes? That would make his feet more attractive than those of a seven-foot tall NBA star!

Men are just as bad. If she isn't packing in the back she doesn't get the time of day, but if she's built like a brick house she can write her own check—or get him to write it.

If that same brick house of a woman has annihilated credit, lives with three kids at her mother's home, unemployed but gets her hair and nails done weekly and has a stank attitude, are you still interested? Probably not.

Life After a Painful Divorce

Balance is best because that figure-eight body may one day be a zero. I did not always have this mind set, but at forty, my thinking has matured. Good sex doesn't make a man commit, but a good woman does. By all means, don't get married because the sex is good. Rather because the relationship is good. If you're connected only because of sex, you will soon become bored with each other. I love fried chicken, but every day; all day. Can someone say salmon, please?

Women will go to great lengths to improve bedroom skills, but never consider enhancing the total package. I have never heard my friends say, "I'm going to marry that woman. She has the best stuff I've ever had." The list of attributes below—not in any particular order—describe my idea of an attractive woman:

- morals
- cleanliness—the literal and figurative temple
- good-paying job
- good credit
- a car
- education
- respectable children

No one knows what you like as much as you do. By all means if you like dark men, go for what you know. If you've always been attracted to light-skinned women, do you. Don't let anyone make you feel bad about your preferences. Parents and pastors sometimes make a drastic mistake in this aspect. They often have good insight, but in the final analysis you have to be attracted to the physical, spiritual, emotional and intellectual character of that individual.

I wouldn't consider marriage with any woman without first seeing these four records:

1. Criminal. These days who you see is not who you get. You can view someone's criminal record for free or a few pennies on the Internet. You can be dating the check-fraud queen and not even know it. He can be a dope dealer with a rap sheet as long as your arm but his warm smile and endless gifts have blinded you. And to single women with daughters; how horrified would you be to learn that your man is a pedophile two years into him molesting your daughter? It would take all day to tell you about people who thought they were dating Dr. Jeckyl, but all along he was Mr. Hyde. Anyone who objects to you seeing their criminal record…you eject!
2. Medical. Have you thought about being married to a sick person? High blood pressure, sugar diabetes or worse, some incurable sexual disease. She may be barren and you want a child. Or a man who can't (Lord, help me) get it up because of his blood pressure. Houston, we have a problem! This matter may seem dismal, but if you become the primary caregiver to your mate, you will realize the importance. From sleepwalking to chronic insomnia, you should be privy to the health of your future mate.
3. Driving record. Road rage, drunk driving or a tendency to run stop signs. If you're the one who's in the car then all of that matters. As a passenger on dates, I have felt like I wouldn't make it out of the car alive. I have a female friend who went on a date and by the time they arrived at the movie theatre, she got out of the car crying and shaking screaming, "Never again." With the high incidences of car crashes, your companion's driving record is essential. A poor driving history can double your premium, when added

to your insurance policy. I know married couples who had to get separate policies for that exact reason. By all means know what you're getting into, before you get into that car!
4. Credit Report. The Bible says that the wicked borrow and do not repay (paraphrased from Psalm 37:21). When you are with a dishonest person, life can be challenging. It is one thing to have a situation that has a negative impact on your credit, but it's another thing when derogatory credit is characteristic of your financial decisions. Connecting with an individual with a shady financial past will create long-term problems in a relationship. Who wants to deal with late payments, screening calls for creditors or hiding the car in your cousin's garage to avoid the repo man? Let me clarify that bad credit doesn't make the person bad. Many good people have made financial mistakes out of ignorance, immaturity or impulse. It is awesome to see an individual repairing their credit with payments to their creditors, downsizing to a more affordable home or changing vehicles to better manage the payment. If you're forty, vacationing and splurging on shopping sprees with a pile of bills on your kitchen table, that's ludicrous. Trust me when I tell you… romance with bad finance is a nuisance.

Chapter 9
Rated R

As a single man, the opportunities for a woman, wife or boo are limitless. At last count, I estimated ten women to every man. Taking into consideration the number of men on drugs, unemployed, incarcerated or with a propensity for fondness of other men, a "good" man is a rare find. Some men use this uniqueness to their advantage at the expense of women's self-esteem.

When I first divorced, I dated as often as possible. All sizes, shapes and educational backgrounds were accessible to me. I saw more of my city in those few years—movie theatres, jazz lounges, ice-cream parlors and restaurants—then I did in the thirteen years I was married. Like Ricky Martin sang, a brother was living la vida loca!

I believed that the plethora of women would sooth my sore heart. I convinced myself that although my wife didn't want to be bothered with me, these women did.

When the benevolent women heard my story and empathized with my pain, they gave me all they had to offer. My boys and I ate like celebrities with a different gourmet chef preparing each meal. Offers for clothes, cash and unmentionables soon followed. I did an occasional chest check to make sure that a bull's eye hadn't been plastered on me. Beyond assertive to aggressive – an unfamiliar territory for a pursuer like myself. I didn't expect the cat to chase the dog. What in the world? Beautiful women with fascinating careers, homes, cars—the total package—in hot pursuit of me.

Marriage is Honorable

When I spoke in Louisville, Kentucky a few years ago, a young lady approached me after service. She pulled me to the side and told me that she enjoyed oral sex with her husband, but her pastor said that it was wrong. The next words she said dumbfounded me.

"So what should I do, Preacher?"

I respect pastors and the rules established for their congregation. I did not want to negate his instruction, but I didn't want her husband waiting for me in the parking lot either. I'll treat the balance of our conversation as a patient-therapist session and not divulge the details of my advice.

As a member of a church presided by Bishop Buckwild, his teachings on marital sex may be based on the following Scripture:

> *Marriage is honorable in all and the bed undefiled.*
> Hebrews 13:4

His philosophy: do what pleases you as long as you both consent to it.

Whereas Bishop Boring adheres to missionary-position-only sex. From his perspective, all else is taboo and an abomination to God. Do you satisfy your companion's desires to keep your marriage flourishing or do you let your pastor run your master bedroom? Think about it.

A Human Magnet

As a traveling minister, I had no idea that speaking to a congregation of believers was an aphrodisiac for women. I'm still not clear why a man of God bringing forth the Word is sexually arousing—an obvious woman thing—but I've been told that a preacher's tone, moves and sweat stimulate women. They daydream about intimate relations while he's winding up his homiletics.

Being divorced made it difficult at times by all the attention I was getting. I got winks, lip-licking and uncrossed legs while I preached the Gospel. The behavior became the norm. I received as many offers for sex as I did for a glass of water.

It is common for women to follow the car of the preacher after church to find out the hotel in which he's staying. Crazy, but true. I've checked into many hotels using an alias to maintain privacy.

Thank God for my father's leadership and a consistent prayer life. I needed both to dodge the advances. The attraction had nothing to do with my physical attributes or evangelistic savvy, but rather the enemy's attempts to thwart my purpose and make a mockery of God.

Some men use their influence to pick up women. I am by no means a goody-two-shoes—some days are better than others—but manipulation has never been my proclivity. Thank the Lord!

It is not the absence of a wedding ring, but the anointing that creates the magnetism. What some women don't know is that most preachers have PMS—prophetic mood swings. We can drive a sister nuts. Ask any first lady.

Life After a Painful Divorce

Masturbation

While no specific Scripture exists on self gratification, doctrines regarding masturbation vary. On countless occasions, I've been asked if it is acceptable to masturbate to avoid fornication. One school of thought teaches that as long as you do not involve another person, you are free to pleasure your flesh. But what about sinning against your body?

> *For ye are bought with a price: therefore glorify God in your body, and in your spirit, which are God's.*
> I Corinthians 6:20

If you fantasize about a partner while you masturbate, haven't you sinned?

> *But I say unto you, that whosoever looketh on a woman to lust after her hath committed adultery with her already in his heart.*
> Matthew 5:28

With sex in your heart and fantasies bombarding your thoughts, the continual longing intensifies. Like Pandora's Box—once opened it is difficult to shut—masturbation often leads to sex with a partner.

Chapter 10
Should I Look For Another or Stay By Myself?

I've asked myself and have been asked this same question by others on a constant basis. The answer changes depending on what's going on in my life and in the lives of others around me.

In a time when people are connecting for all the wrong reasons: loneliness, desperation, parenting assistance, finances; I recognized that loneliness for a season is far better than misery for a lifetime.

I have witnessed humdrum relationships that led to affairs, pornography addictions or two people co-existing under one roof. At the sports bar, he's watching the game, while she's chatting on her cell phone. In the mall, he's heading to Radio Shack, while she's rushing to Macy's. They coordinate a meeting time and place as if they were on a field trip. They might as well be alone by the way they disregard each other's presence. They have grown accustomed to the predictable, monotonous routine.

People connect for all the wrong reasons: loneliness, desperation, help with their kids, help paying their bills and social status. Being lonely for a season is far better than being miserable for a lifetime.

The challenge is to have patience to deal with the season of loneliness whether six months or six years. Dating can be interesting and fascinating: meeting people from different walks, going to new places, dining at exquisite restaurants. Those things can keep you dating

Life After a Painful Divorce

for years, only if it went like that. No one talks about the idiosyncrasies hidden in the middle. You don't know that he rented the BMW or that she's still dating a felon who's been following you all night. Or what about the forty-year-old brother who took the pictures off the wall before you came over so you wouldn't know that he lives with his mother?

If you don't have discernment, you can burn out quickly. My father used to ask me, "Why continue to date someone with whom you know you have no future?"

People will date you, spend your money, run you across town on errands, all the while knowing that you are a temporary stand-in until the real mate comes along. One of the most sincere things an individual can do is set the boundaries at the beginning of the relationship. Be honest about your intentions whether you're looking for occasional companionship or a lifelong commitment.

Let me caution you. Although you state and reiterate your plan, after a few dates it is not uncommon for feelings to supersede logic. That's when problems arise. As a mature adult, you may have to put your feelings in check and say, "I need to abort this relationship because I'm getting in over my head." Don't look for the other person to control the relationship. If your feelings have unleashed and you don't harness the reigns, you will get hurt. An immature individual will accuse the other person of "playing with my emotions" and place the blame on the wrong party. One psychologist said, "When a person tells you how they feel, believe them." I agree.

I experienced the excruciating pain of rejection when my ex-wife first asked for a divorce. I thought we could work through our differences. I got on my knees and begged her to stay. Her refusal was one of the most hurtful blows to my ego. Even as I wrote this chapter—years after the divorce—I cringe at the memory. A spirit of rejection came upon me causing me to terminate many blossoming relationships. I'm sure my abrupt actions left some wondering, "What in the world did I do wrong?"

They That Wait Upon the Lord

I learned to wait. Time allowed me to endure special days, holidays and celebrations alone. I used the time to develop, grow and understand me.

My mother taught me how to cook chicken, macaroni and cheese, pecan cornbread and more. I enjoyed the delight in my sons' eyes when they came home from school and inhaled the aroma of homemade dinner. Pride engulfed me when they requested specific meals I had prepared, especially fried fish. I designated Wednesday nights as Mexican Night with fajitas, tacos and picanté sauce.

I have always taken my mother out to lunch, however following the divorce, our excursions were like counseling sessions. If you want to know about women, talk to a woman and likewise for men. My mother imparted fresh wisdom. She told me that a man should not be totally dependent on a woman for anything but reproduction. Know how to wash your clothes, clean your home, iron and plant flowers in a garden if that's your thing. I believe she could have been a psychiatrist or hosted a talk show.

As the light that once shined brightly, again peeked from my soul, I asked the question: why take the actions of one woman out on all women? I have a better understanding about women. For example, it's natural for a woman to want—and expect—security from a man, a sense of belonging.

> *But they that wait upon the Lord shall renew their strength. They shall mount up with wings, as eagles; they shall run and not be weary and they shall walk and not faint.*
> Isaiah 40:31

For years, I pondered whether I was willing to risk rejection again. The potential for a relationship to end on bad terms is ever-prevalent. Fear of failure stands side-by-side with rejection. This spirit must be conquered by the Word of God and prayer. Rejection is not a bad thing if your desires are not the desires God has for you. I'm learning that man's rejection is God's protection. Our finite minds cannot conceptualize that his omniscience means that He's looking out for our best interest even though we can't see the future.

I know church girls who were attracted to thugs. Only after they acted upon the attraction and attached to the hoodlums did they realize the mistake. God caused that thug to reject you because his next woman received a three-year-prison sentence for carrying drugs in her car. It could have been you. I have friends who have been rejected by women—whom they loved and cherished—for someone who made more money. Once they got over the humiliation and hurt, they realized that God did them a favor. Who wants a gold digger as a companion?

It took me three years to thank my ex-wife for divorcing me. Her actions made me the man I am today; better and ten times stronger. Stop crying and stressing about who rejected you. It's part of God's plan to make you better not bitter.

> *The stone which the builders rejected has become the chief cornerstone.*
> I Peter 2:7 NKJV

Your heart may be broken in a hundred pieces because of the person who left you for someone else, but I dare you to keep living. You will see it was a backdoor blessing. Take that pain and make it work for you. Draw something positive from the relationship: a better understanding of your expectations, a different way to communicate, third-eye vision for spotting future counterfeits. Since it didn't destroy you, it served to make you stronger.

Do me a favor: put down this book and write a note to someone who rejected you. In a sweet spirit—no sarcasm—thank that person for the times you had. Indicate something positive that you learned during the relationship. Express how you are excited about the next chapter in your life. Purge yourself of the baggage of unfinished business. You can forward the note to them or discard it. It's the act of releasing the pain and taking back your peace of mind that's essential to this favor. I promise the lightened burden will feel like you dropped a backpack of bricks after a three-mile hike…up hill! Keep in mind that if you feel the urge to cuss them out or belittle their character, you are not ready to do me this favor. Take more time to heal and regroup.

Life After a Painful Divorce

Can I Divorce-Proof My Marriage?

Ultimately, only God knows if a marriage is divorce-proof as only He can look into the heart. For whatever reason, many people—especially Christians—believe that marriage generates an automatic divorce-proof mechanism. Whether faith or ignorance, they do not expect their marriage to fail and so they do not put adequate effort into making it succeed. The end result, as stated earlier, is an abnormally high incidence of divorce in Christian marriages. Like a scout trekking the marshes as front man for his platoon, they were ambushed by enemies camouflaged and laying in wait.

> *But he that is married careth for the things that are of the world, how he may please his wife.*
> I Corinthians 7:33

As quiet as it's kept, marriage is not about you. Rather it is about how much you can care for and love your spouse. If all married persons were giving and unselfish with respect to their mates, the divorce rate would plummet.

I meet single people who have developed a list of stipulations for their pending prisoner—I mean mate. With preconceived notions and limitations on the depth of their love, they have plagued the relationship before it begins.

A successful marriage is without barriers. How can two become one with mountains of differences distancing them?

Like Christ loves us without limits, so should you love your mate. Be willing to do whatever it takes to support, love and satisfy your mate or do not get married. You are not ready if your needs supersede those of your partner.

Expert marriage counselors give two main reasons for the infidelity of men: they are not stimulated in the bedroom or the boardroom. The bedroom is self-explanatory: we want what we want, when we want it. Women tend to give what they want, when they want and how they want to give it. If a man asks for a glass of orange juice and you give him a glass of milk, have you met his need? Sure he may no longer be thirsty, but the desire has not been quenched.

The boardroom equates to the emotional needs of a man—that's right, men have feelings too. A man wants to feel like the king of the jungle, the leader of the pack, the head of his home. He wants his wife to admire him, adore him and stroke his ego on occasion. God wired us this way. That's why He commanded women to reverence their husbands in Ephesians 5. A man's need to be revered or respected is like a woman's need to be loved. Without it, we are empty.

As creatures of habit, it is difficult to modify behavior once it has been reinforced by repetition. However, marriage is about flexibility. Forget the cliché: it's a give and take. Give without concern for the return and watch what happens.

So can you divorce proof your marriage? Open communication, quality time and selflessness are great tools to safeguard your marriage, but only God knows the intent of the heart. Seek Him diligently. Ask Him to show you the heart of your beloved and once He exposes the truth, believe it.

Sometimes Opposites Attack

Some people say that opposites attract, but they can also attack. When individuals try to get to know one another, it is an exchange of information. You are finding out new and different things about that person. Sometimes their lifestyle is in total contrast to yours—interesting at first but can later become a source of contention if you are not open for change. It is unfair to put enormous expectations on a person to change to accommodate your preferences. Change occurs from the inside out and only if desired by the changer.

I'm learning that many people live within parenthesis. They seldom leave their side of town, go to the same grocery store, shop at the same malls, etc. Creatures of habit confined within a self-imposed box. I know people who take the same route to and from work; never venturing a different way for a change of scenery.

If you connect with someone you like but don't like their ways, problems will arise. Anyone can act like they enjoy your lifestyle when what they enjoy is you. The two likes are not the same. For example; he is into horror and action movies, when you enjoy romance and comedies. Your initial fondness for him will have you seated in the theatre shielding your eyes and screaming when the slow-running woman falls for the fifth time and the ax-wielding psychopath slices her like a tomato. But after a few decapitations and dismemberments, you encourage him to see that with his friends. Many men—me included—do not like to go shopping with women; mother, sister or girlfriend. Deception will have me at the mall with her, full smile, carrying bags, as if I'm enjoying our fellowship. Eight months later—when I have been in every store at least ten times—I express my true feelings. From her perspective, I have changed, when in fact I'm reverting to my true self. If you don't care for certain things, let it be known up front.

Flaws and All

Some differences are manageable while others are unacceptable to you. Should you accept flaws and all? A classy woman would not tolerate a manner-less man. His lack of etiquette would cause her too much embarrassment. A financially-astute man will struggle in a relationship with a woman who spends her mortgage money on stilettos and weekly hair appointments.

I have a friend who had taken his woman-friend and her son to the movies. In route to the theatre, her son kicked the back of the driver's seat in rhythm with the music. He waited to see if his date would correct her child, but she said nothing. Fifteen minutes into the kangarooing, he turned down the music and asked her to have her son stop. She copped an attitude, took on the sister-girl posture and said, "He's only a child, so stop tripping." He was driving a $60,000 S-Class Mercedes with six motors in the seat. But even if he had a Chevy Chevette, the fact that she did not require her son to respect his property remained. This incident led to their breakup.

A major flaw many daters overlook—because they are so caught up in each other—is the flaw of children. Before you turn me off, let me clarify. Studies have been proven that children can be the main reason for the demise of a relationship. Discipline, differing expectations, child support and dealing with the drama of the other parent can run off the weak at heart. If these components are not addressed, the relationship is doomed.

Allergic to Kids

If you have children—and the person you are dating acts allergic to them—that's a serious problem. How do you overcome that hurdle? The opposing sides should be a deal breaker, but some people are so preoccupied with companionship that they allow their children to be mistreated. I know a guy whose new wife told him that his twelve-year-old daughter can visit for a few hours but never spend the night. He agreed despite the fact that they have two spare bedrooms and a huge backyard. A parent who allows this type of treatment is not worthy of a child.

Dating a person who also has kids can be a plus as they are more apt to understand the dynamics of effective parenting. Plans change in a matter of minutes because a child has a stomach ache or the baby sitter forgot you needed her services. If you have well-mannered kids and your love interest doesn't care for kids, like a doctor in the delivery room holding a newborn, cut the cord.

How Bad Do You Want It?

"How bad do you want it?" is a viable question that must be asked in your quest for companionship. Will you accept a studio apartment, tolerate a twenty-year-old hoopty or endure cheap polyester clothes off the clearance rack? Or do you draw the line at a three-bedroom house, a BMW and custom-tailored clothes? Most never ask that question because they think that love is sufficient.

> *Can two walk together, except they be agreed?*
> Amos 3:3

Some people are content living at the bottom of the barrel, while others never settle for second best. Is this conundrum love or war? Your aspirations, goals and ambitions need to be comparable for the relationship to flourish. You need to consider where they are today, where they desire to be in the future and how that fits into your plans. What's wrong with wanting to live in a $300,000 house if you're willing to work for it? Is it wrong to want three automobiles or vacation four weeks a year? Don't connect with someone who's content living with a basement mentality, when God has ordained you to possess the penthouse.

Cleanliness is Next to Godliness

Psychologists say that if you want to know if you can get along with a person, live with them. You'd never know that the man who picks you up in a clean car with polished shoes, fresh haircut and minty-fresh breath, keeps his house in such disarray that it needs to be condemned. French-tip nails, red lipstick and green eye shadow can mask her unkempt house that reeks of two-week-old dishes, piles of dirty clothes and used kitty litter.

Cleanliness is next to Godliness. It's not a Scripture but it's true nonetheless. You can have enough love in your relationship to fill every cabin on the Love Boat, but if your love interest has bad living habits, you're in for a rumble in the jungle. I had a friend who didn't like going home because his house was filthy. He refused to make

Life After a Painful Divorce

love to his wife until she cleaned the house. That's crazy. Know what you're working with. Stop by—unannounced—to see how they keep the house. Anyone can clean up when they know you're visiting, but what about when they aren't expecting you? Can you live with a man who leaves his underwear on the living room floor, lets the trashcan flow over like Niagara Falls and only flushes when he defecates? I know it's a little disgusting, but I know a guy with the toilet mentality: If it's yellow, let it mellow. If it's brown; flush it down. Yuck! I used the bathroom in the home of a female friend. The sink had so much hair in it that it looked like a chia pet got a haircut.

On the other end of the spectrum, we have the super clean freaks: obsessed with cleaning to the point that it becomes unbearable. Vacuuming the same room four times a day to remove footprints or emptying the trash when a paper towel is dropped in it can be a bit much. Look for balance in someone with habits similar to yours. The commonality does not mean that things will flow smoothly, but at least you have minimized a potential source of disruption.

<u>Commitment</u>

Committing when so many options are presented is difficult. Think of it as being confined in a town jail when cowboys, saloons and gun fights were prevalent. The sheriff's feet are propped on the desk. His head bobs as he nods off to sleep. You see your chance for freedom on the wall where the cell keys hang on a hook just beyond your reach. Who wants to be chained to the wrong person when the possibility of mutual fulfillment is inches away?

I realize that I may never get everything I want from one woman; however some things are non-negotiable (see the chapter *Delivered from Divorce* for my list of preferences).

At times, my desire is to remain single. The freedom to come and go at my discretion is attractive. Bringing a wife into the picture can lead to disagreements about time, interests and money. I am comfortable watching every televised sporting event on my big screen TV with the volume on blast, eating dinner without vegetables and sleeping across the width of my bed.

The singleness decision can put a man on the top of every woman's list. Women can be quite aggressive and that posturing feeds the flames of an already hot situation.

To the single and ready-to-mingle crew, be true, honest and forthright with whom you are dating. If you play games be prepared for the penalty: sugar in the gas tank, keyed car, a brick through the picture window, harassing phone calls and more. If you see the relationship going no further than an occasional casual dinner, make that known in the beginning.

Some daters are too impatient to take the time to know you and let you know them. A third-date female said to me, "You need to tell me now; where is this relationship going?"

After a slight chuckle, I said, "To a movie and then getting some chicken wings." No fourth date with her.

From my experience, women read more into a friendship than men. He invites her to a family function to hang out and she perceives it as acceptance into the family. He asks her to join him for dinner (he has to eat so why not have some company); she considers it a date.

Life After a Painful Divorce

I recommend an outing to the movies or a not-so-quaint restaurant in the platonic, friendly, get-to-know-this-person phase of the relationship to keep things impersonal.

To avoid the deadly descent into the abyss of craziness, even when a man is bored and she wants to connect daily, don't walk toward the light. Once you set a precedence of routine time together—in person, by telephone or text—be mindful that your "friend" may equate time spent as a call for commitment. Let your words and actions complement each other and convey your intentions on a regular basis. Otherwise, he or she may accuse you of leading them on. This technique may not work for everyone; that's why you have the option of filing a restraining order. Now that's funny.

Chapter 11
Delivered from Divorce

On the thirteenth anniversary of my wedding—July 25—my divorce was final. The day it began was the same day it ended. Interesting, huh? My lifelong commitment to love, honor and respect, began and ended on the same day.

Someone asked, "If you had to do it all over again, would you?"

Without hesitation, I said, "Yes." Despite the heartache, the marriage had high points: two wonderful sons, a deeper knowledge of self, good people on her side of the family, etc.

I do not harbor any ill feelings. My ex-wife and I have our moments, but overall it's good. We *chose* to maintain a mature relationship for our children. We collectively decided that our sons deserved two civil parents who could be in the same room without arguing or "showing out" all while expressing unconditional love for them. We made sure that the boys understood the divorce was not their fault. It took some time, but the sadness I once saw in my sons' eyes is gone. I like that.

The Transition

My ex-wife has since left Christianity. She studies Islam and is now Muslim. I wondered if she ever believed like I did—given the bipolarization between doctrines—but left that judgment for the Lord. The boys complain because they are not allowed to order pepperoni or sausage on pizza when they visit with her, but they make up for it when they get home. I have no problem with pork on my fork. The pork matter sounds trivial, but it's the subtle—and often overlooked—differences that can hinder the transition even between amicable parents. The mind is an amazing organ. It adapts to overwhelming situations—and by the grace of God—makes you do the seemingly impossible. Many people told me that they could not have endured a divorce without unleashing rage or numbing the pain with alcohol and drugs. The best lesson I learned about love and women is that you never know what you can endure until you have to endure it. And because I'm a fast learner, the mistakes that I made out of ignorance and immaturity will not be repeated.

Who's Next?

Should the Lord opt for me to marry again, I will not jump into it on the hopes that she has the potential to meet my needs and will change in the areas that lack. I have assessed some characteristics—must-haves and preferences. Be ye also ready.

ಒ A communicator. My lady friend has to be open to interactive dialogue. Not one who shuts down and locks me out when she's upset. Communication means to reach a common ground or level of understanding. That cannot happen if one of the two involved is not engaged in the discussion.

ಒ Submissive. The ten-letter profane word that women dread and some men abuse. Submission is biblical and reciprocal: "Submit yourselves one to another," so why shy away from it? I'm not looking to launch an argument over every decision. Loud, overbearing, bossy is not a fit for me. Can she be assertive? Yes. Aggressive? Not in the least. A refined, witty woman who can get what she wants without putting her hands on her hips and her finger in my face.

- Feminine. I am a saved man, but a man nonetheless. I want my woman to look like a woman. Her sway, her scent, her hair. W-o-m-a-n. Enough said.
- Giving. My lady has to have a giving spirit which includes understanding and responding to my needs: giving me what I want and not what she wants me to have. Get your mind out of the gutter.
- Secure. My wife needs to know that she's all I want and need. By the time I lavish her with my kindness, affection and whatever else makes her feel loved, she will not have to question her position as my "one and only."
- Alive. No, not as in breathing, but living life. As a speaker, I am on the go quite a bit. I need my woman to have a life that fulfills and occupies her. I am not built to have someone follow me around like a parole officer. Of course our life together will be top priority but I want her to have interests of her own.
- Employment. Lord, please let her have a job and accomplishments beyond a lofty wardrobe. My bachelor friends explained that a woman who has not acquired anything is a "shell woman." She is shaped just right, long hair, perfect complexion, sexy smile, yet she has no money, no job, lives with three girlfriends in a two-bedroom apartment and has a funky attitude. Taking on the form of woman-ness, but denying the virtue thereof. This type of woman is dateable when you're bored but she'd never get a

Life After a Painful Divorce

chance to meet your church family and definitely not your mother. Her value is limited to one room of the house and I do not mean the kitchen.

- ☙ A 401k plan, good credit and respectable children—along with appealing physical attributes—round out my wonderful woman.
- ☙ God-fearing. My betrothed must have a personal relationship with the Lord that permeates throughout her life. A worshipper at church, home and work. I am in church every Sunday and oftentimes several days through the week. The relationship won't work if I want to worship and she wants to club it.

> *Favor is deceitful and beauty is vain, but a woman that feareth the Lord shall be praised.*
> Proverbs 30:31

I know it's a lot to ask, but since I'm going to wait I might as well wait for what I want.

Three days after I met one young lady, she said, "I'm so glad I met you. I'm three months behind on my car note."

With my eyebrows raised, I said, "And what does that have to do with me?"

How is it that a woman wants a commitment but has nothing to commit? Finding a woman who wants you for you—and not what you have—is harder than finding a pair of Pradas at K-Mart. I understand that most women want security, but when a man sets the table with plates and silverware and she doesn't bring anything for the meal but an appetite, it doesn't make for a good presentation.

Men are even receptive to a progressive woman who has not yet "arrived." Attending college or trade school, repairing her credit or in a first-time-home-buyer's program speaks volumes. Working toward improvement is a turn on for me.

The Bounce-Back Factor

Through hard work and the blessings of God I have rebounded in several aspects. Financially, I make on-time mortgage payments and have three reliable vehicles—S500 Mercedes, Navigator and a late-model Camry—all paid-in-full.

My boys have the same pre-divorce bedrooms with Fathead posters of their favorite athletes plastered on the walls. They still shoot hoops on the basketball court in the yard and for eight years running we take an annual summer vacation to Orlando, Florida.

I'm enjoying more personal travel too. New York, Detroit and Atlanta are favorite destinations and I recently added a new outlet. Scuba diving in Barbados is one of the most exhilarating things I have ever experienced.

My favorite spot is the backyard gazebo; lying in my lounge chair with the fireplace simmering.

But my most prized possession is peace of mind. I never expected to have true peace given the trauma and drama of the divorce. From the other side of understanding, I encourage you to seek peace above everything else and the rest will follow.

> *Seek peace and ensue it.*
> I Peter 3:11

Life After a Painful Divorce

The following three points have put a smile on my face, hope in my heart and reassurance in my spirit:
1. Accept what has happened
2. Let it go
3. Believe the best is yet to come

When you accept the situation, you align yourself with the will of God.

While in prayer, God said to me, "*I allowed it because I knew you could handle it.*"

Whether you have been fired, evicted or your children are on assignment from satan, God knew it before it happened and still allowed it. Destiny does not only work for good things, but the bad also. A drive-by shooting, a home invasion or an eighteen-month stint in jail is part of your destiny, if God allows it.

I once said, "I wish I had never married."

God asked me, "*Do you really believe that?*" Of course He knew the answer. I believe that He wanted me to hear how foolish I sounded.

I picked up my cell phone, looked at my sons on the wallpaper and said, "Lord, I hear You." If life experiences form character, then you must ask; was it worth it? Absolutely.

What makes me jump out of bed without an alarm clock? The knowledge that better is in my future. Somewhere someone is moving into their dream home, opening a business, driving off the lot in a new vehicle or marrying their soul mate. If it's happening to someone, why can't it happen to you? God walked you through it and the best is yet to come. Receive it. You survived a momentous life-changing event. Walk tall—chest out, head high, shoulders squared—because you are a survivor. Live knowing that your happiness is not determined by a ring on your finger or by who has left your life. Your happiness is in knowing that you are here for a reason. Not to just endure pain and suffering, but to have joy and happiness. And after coming through a rough season, you certainly qualify for years of smooth sailing on a boat named Peace. Ride on my friends and know that there is *Life After a Painful Divorce*.

End Notes

[1] http://en.wikipedia.org/wiki/Johari_Window

[2] http://en.wikipedia.org/wiki/Pygmalion_Effect

About Jonathan K. Sanders

One of eight children born to Bishop Fred and Esther Sanders, Jonathan realized there was a call on his life at an early age. Even though the enemy planned to deter the young evangelist from reaching his destiny, God's plan would ultimately prevail. After years of struggling with drugs, alcohol abuse and crime, the Lord delivered Jonathan through a revival conducted by his father on September 28, 1990 in Detroit, Michigan.

J. K. Sanders' unique deliverance ministry has transformed lives and caused souls to be set free. Anointed with the gift of prophecy, he utters the oracles of God with accuracy. His intense delivery of the Gospel will grip your spirit and challenge your intellect with sermons such as *I Survived a Bad Experience* and *How to Act When Under Attack*.

A living testimony that the power of God can deliver and transform, he preaches the Gospel with authority, standing boldly on his favorite Scripture:

What shall we then say to these things? If God be for us, who can be against us? ~Romans 8:31

For more information about Jonathan K. Sanders visit

JKSandersMinistries.org.

FaceBook.com/JonathanKSanders

Life After a Painful Divorce

Queen V Publishing
The Doorway to YOUR Destiny!

Go thou and publish abroad the kingdom of God.
—Luke 9:60

We are a Christian contract publisher committed to transforming manuscripts into polished works of art. **Queen V Publishing**—a company of standard and integrity—offers an alternative that allows God's word in YOU to do what it was sent to do for OTHERS.

Visit the website for complete guidelines on manuscript submission and the plan that best fits your literary goals.

QueenVPublishing.net

We help experts master self-publishing!

Valerie L. Coleman
Dayton, Ohio
937.307.0760
Info@PenoftheWriter.com

Blended Families An Anthology
A Black Christian Book Distributors and Christian Small Publishers Association Bestseller!

By Valerie L. Coleman

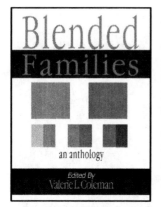

ISBN-13: 978-0-9786066-0-2

With divorce, single-parent households and family crises on the rise, many people are experiencing the tumultuous dynamics of stepfamilies. Learn biblical principles and practical tools to help your family thrive. ***Blended Families An Anthology*** ministers to the needs of those hurting and crying out for answers.

We are **not** the Brady Bunch!

Tainted Mirror An Anthology
By Valerie L. Coleman

ISBN: 978-0-9786066-1-9

What's keeping you from your destiny?

Whether restricted by prison walls, the influence of others or held hostage by self-inflicted limitations, captivity starts in the mind. We allow our thoughts to create virtual restrainers that stifle our dreams and hinder our purpose.

Based on I Corinthians 13:12, ***Tainted Mirror An Anthology*** offers stories of hope and healing to overcome the mental, physical and emotional strongholds that keep us from fulfilling our destiny.

Available on **Amazon.com, BlackCBD.com** and
PenoftheWriter.com

Life After a Painful Divorce

For speaking engagements or to order additional copies of

Life After a Painful Divorce

Jonathan K Sanders Ministries, LLC
1933 East Dublin Granville Road #237
Columbus, Ohio 43229
614.840.9141
JKSandersMinistries.org
JSanders1718@yahoo.com

* * * * * * * * * * * * * * * * *

Please mail _____ copies of
Life After a Painful Divorce

Name _____

Address _____

City / State / Zip _____
(____)_____
Phone

Email _____

Quantity	Price Per Book	Total
	$14.95	
Sales Tax (Ohio residents add $1.05 per book)		
Shipping ($1.99 first book, $0.99 each additional)		
Grand Total* (Payable to: Jonathan K. Sanders)		

* Certified check and money orders only

Also available on Amazon.com